Exemplary Leadership

A Practical Approach Into

Exemplary Leadership

By
Major T. Beesley

Beesley Books Edition

Printed in the United States of America

First Printing: March 2017

Book Description

Leadership.

A process whereby a person uses his/her capacity to inspire, spur and impact others to accomplish an objective and coordinates the organization in a way that makes it more cognizant and firm.

Leadership happens within the setting of a group, it includes affecting others, it is a procedure, and it involves objective achievement and the objectives are shared by leaders and their followers.

The very demonstration of defining leadership as a procedure proposes that leadership is not a characteristic or trait with which just a couple of certain individuals are enriched with during childbirth.

Characterizing leadership as a procedure implies that leadership is a transactional occasion that happens between leaders and their followers.

Seeing leadership as a procedure implies that leaders influence and are influenced by their followers either positively or negatively.

It emphasizes that leadership is a two-way, intuitive occasion between leaders and followers rather than a linear, one-way occasion in which the leader just influences the followers.

Characterizing leadership as a procedure makes it accessible not only to a chosen few but to anyone who chooses to follow it.

More important, it implies that leadership is not just confined to the one individual in a group who has formal and/or positional power.

People can learn leadership skills.

People can choose to become leaders.

This is widely accepted today and is the premise on which this guide is based.

In these pages you will learn:

- **What Leadership Truly is**
- **The Differences Between Various Types of Leadership**
- **The Traits of Good Leaders**
- **The Differences Between Managers and Leaders**
- **Steps to Becoming a Leader**
- **And much, much more!**

Contents

Chapter 4: Leaders/Managers

1. Managers
2. Leaders

Chapter 5: Leadership In Business

1. Anticipate
2. Challenge
3. Interpret
4. Decide
5. Align
6. Learn
7. Family Leadership
8. Community Leadership

Chapter 6: Attributes Or 'Personality Traits' Of Good Leaders

1. Vigorous & Enthusiastic
2. Charming
3. Open
4. Self-Motivated
5. Committed
6. Future-Oriented
7. Intelligent
8. Purpose Driven
9. Open To Change
10. Inclusive
11. Focus
12. Learn From Mistakes
13. Ethical
14. Self-Control
15. Adversity Quotient And Leaders

Chapter 7: Steps To Great Leadership

1. Understand Yourself
2. Understand Your Followers
3. Understand The Situation
4. Communication
5. Encourage Enthusiasm And A Sense Of Belonging
6. Keep Everyone Working On Agreed Upon Objectives
7. Treat Others As Individuals. Put Your Knowledge And Understanding Of Each Group Member To Work!
8. Accept Responsibility For Getting Things Done
9. Master Your Emotions

Chapter 8: Six Common Challenges Leaders Face Across Seven Countries

1. Developing Managerial Effectiveness
2. Inspiring Others
3. Developing Employees
4. Leading A Team
5. Guiding Change
6. Managing Politics And Internal Stakeholders

Conclusion

Dear Friends,

Dreamers are separated from doers by their level of commitment.

It is to the soldier, going over the slope, not realizing what's waiting on the opposite side.

It is to the boxer getting off the mat once again after having been thumped down.

It is to the marathon runner, pushing another ten miles even after their strength is no more.

It is to the leader, all that and more in light of the fact that everyone you lead is relying upon you.

Never stop dreaming.

Best of choices,

Major Theodore Beesley

INTRODUCTION

For over a thousand years, the subject of leadership has been of interest from the early Greek philosophers, such as Socrates and Plato, to the leadership masters whose books fill airport bookshops and plenty of managers' bookshelves. However, the desire for effective leadership has seldom been more emphatically voiced than now. In this changing world, it is argued that leadership holds not just the answers to the success of sectors and regions, organizations, and people, but to countries as well and to the holistic world. However, questions remain as to what leadership really is or how to characterize it.

Research and practice of leadership is ever expanding, though there are stumps that hamper them. Leadership has been kept in certain mystery regardless of the recognition of its importance. Two fundamental challenges lie at the heart of the issue of defining leadership. Firstly, leadership is a complex construct open to subjective translations like ideas such as 'happiness', 'love' and, 'freedom'. Based on a mixture of learning and experience, everybody has their own intuitive comprehension as to what leadership is, which is in a concise definition difficult to capture. Secondly, one's hypothetical stance strongly influences the way in which leadership is comprehended and defined.

There are individuals who view leadership as a social procedure that rises from group relationships whilst others view leadership as the consequence of a set of characteristics possessed by 'leaders'. Such disparate views about the nature of leadership will always bring about in a difference of opinion. Many theories and formal models are there which look to identify the key behaviors and characteristics that help leaders to succeed and it is perhaps more valuable to explore such attributes in everyday terms whilst these are beneficial. It's important in doing so, to understand how skills and traits relate to one another.

Of course, certain skills are vital for leaders, yet without certain personal qualities however, it is impossible for leaders to retain their skills. Few would argue for example, that for leaders, communication skills are vital but no matter what communication skills they learn, if a leader does not have self-control, then they will not be able to apply them because all their best practices will go out the window as soon as they lose their temper. For this reason, you need to reflect on who you are before meditating upon what you do when considering personal leadership effectiveness.

Chapter

1

Leaders and Leadership

CHAPTER 1 – LEADERS AND LEADERSHIP

Leaders are made, not conceived. You can become an effective leader on the off chance that you have the longing and resolution. Through a ceaseless procedure of self-study, training, education, and experience, great leaders develop. Other management concepts such as inspiration, communication, authority, power and delegation are related to leadership. The relationship through which an individual influences the conduct and activities of other individuals is leadership. There are certain things you must be, know, and, do to motivate your followers into higher levels of teamwork. Naturally, these do fall in place but through persistent work and study. To enhance their leadership abilities great leaders are ceaselessly studying and working; they are NOT resting on their laurels.

Leaders ought to make an environment where motivation, honesty, and practical objective setting are present. Elucidation of objectives and communication ought to be persistent. A few leaders, by making members feel that all the achievements realized are a result of a collective effort, cultivate devotion and build up their group.

A few leaders are adroit at permitting followers to come to their own choices and create all alone. They may exercise little power and give next to no direction over the group. There are different sorts of leaders. There are those who may be referred to as democratic. They give direction, offer recommendations, permit the group to arrive at their own particular choices and fortify team member's ideas. There are also the kind of leaders who make all the decisions for the group without their information, set the pace, and look for little approval from colleagues. A full display of legitimate style is taken by this sort of leader in which he or she accepts few suggestions from colleagues and assumes full responsibility for the team member's progress.

Leaders may frequently be characterized by their decisiveness and capacity to steer and inspire others into the accomplishment of a vision. They may be considered as people with the ability to coordinate, control, move or oversee others. We can therefore define a fruitful leader by both their execution, as well as by their acknowledgment of a vision established accomplishment of objectives. This vision ought to be a view of the future that should be shared with the team members.

At the point when a man is choosing on the off chance that she regards you as a leader, she watches what you do as such that she can know who you truly are rather than considering your characteristics, she uses this perception to tell if you are a leader that can be trusted and an honorable leader or a self-serving individual who abuses authority to get advanced and look good. Leaders who are Self-serving are not as compelling on the grounds that their workers do not follow them but only obey them. Since they present a decent picture to their seniors at the detriment of their workers they succeed in many areas.

The premise of great leadership to your organization is selfless service and fair character. Your leadership is all that you do which impacts the organization's objectives and well-being in your workers' eyes. Respected leaders focus on what they are [be] (for example, convictions and character), what they know (for example job, tasks, and human nature), and what they do (for example, implementing, motivating, and providing direction).

What makes a person want to take after a leader? Individuals want those they respect and who have a reasonable ability to know east from west to guide them. They must be ethical to gain admiration. Accomplishing a sense of direction is by passing a solid vision of the future.

Chapter

2

Leadership

CHAPTER 2 – LEADERSHIP

Leadership is a process whereby a person uses his/her capacity to inspire, spur and impact others to accomplish an objective and coordinates the organization in a way that makes it more cognizant and firm. A few components central to the phenomenon of leadership is recommended by this definition.

Some of them are as follows:

(a) Leadership happens within the setting of a group.

(b) Leadership includes affecting others.

(c) Leadership is a procedure

(d) Leadership involves objective achievement.

(e) These objectives are shared by leaders and their followers.

The very demonstration of defining leadership as a procedure proposes that leadership is not a characteristic or trait with which just a couple of certain individuals are enriched with during childbirth. Characterizing leadership as a procedure implies that leadership is a transactional occasion that happens between leaders and their followers. Seeing leadership as a procedure implies that leaders influence and are influenced by their followers either positively or negatively. It emphasizes that leadership is a two-way, intuitive occasion between leaders and followers rather than a linear, one-way occasion in which the leader just influences the followers.

Characterizing leadership as a procedure makes it accessible not only to a chosen few but to everyone who are born with it. More important, it implies that leadership is not just confined to the one individual in a group who has formal position power (i.e., the formally chosen leader). Leadership is about influence, the capacity to influence, in a work or organizational context, your companions, your subordinates, and your superiors. It is not possible to be a leader without influence. Having influence definitely implies that on the part of leaders there is a more prominent need to exercise their influence morally.

Leadership works in groups. This implies that influencing a group of individuals who are occupied in a shared goal or purpose is what leadership is all about. For leaders, this can be a small center to carry out this procedure by applying their leadership characteristics, for example, values, convictions, character, morals, skills and knowledge. In spite of the fact that your position as a supervisor, manager, lead etc. gives you the authority to achieve certain goals in the organization, this power basically makes you the boss, it does not make you a leader.

Leaders work with and make their followers want to achieve high objective contrasts, as opposed to simply bossing around individuals. Additionally, leaders require the confidence to build self-regard in others and still keep a solid level of uprightness in them. With this comes the capacity to impact an organization up, below and laterally as well as externally and internally. One must have the capacity to gain the approval of everyone required to make a thought reality. The leader is denoted by the capacity to be a team player, to create helpful relations and to make an atmosphere that backs a high level of collegiality.

Leadership is tested further by the capacity to frequently, over a drawn out stretch of time, inspire others and guide them successfully. Peter Drucker stated, "Management is doing things right; leadership is doing the right things." The "right" in management terms originates from the association with others. Leadership is a helpful exertion encouraged by listening, gathering a variety of opinions, considering effective strategies and effectively creating an unmistakable vision. It's never an individual's directing. Leadership has a strict meaning of being "the conduct of a person when he is coordinating the exercises of a group towards a shared goal."

It is the "procedure of impacting", toward objective accomplishment, the exercises of a composed group, also, the way towards giving significant direction to collective efforts and accomplishing your goal. In spite of the fact that meanings of what leadership is are great, it basically dependably joins the capacity to influence people with the target of accomplishing proposed objectives. Notwithstanding those set by an organization, a leader needs to accomplish demanding, intense objectives that the leader sets their self and focus on surpassing both goals. It is important to maintain an entrepreneurial spirit as critical as adaptability as it contributes to this condition of leadership.

Leaders may frequently be characterized by their conclusiveness and capacity to control and propel others into the accomplishment of dreams. They may be considered likewise as people with the ability to maneuver, motivate, control, oversee or coordinate others. A fruitful leader might be therefore characterized, not only by their performance, but by their acknowledgment of a dream set up or accomplishment of objectives. This vision ought to be a perspective of the future that ought to be shared with team members.

Bass' (1989 & 1990) Leadership Theory states that, to explain how people become leaders, there are three basic ways. The leadership development for a small number of people is explained by the first two. These theories are:

The Trait Theory:

This theory states that some personality traits may lead people naturally into leadership roles.

The Great Events Theory:

This theory states that a crisis or important event may cause a person to rise to the occasion, which brings out extraordinary leadership qualities in an ordinary person.

The Transformational Leadership Theory:

This theory states that people can learn leadership skills. People can choose to become leaders. It is the most widely accepted theory today and the premise on which this guide is based.

The basis of good leadership is selfless service and honorable character to your organization. Your leadership is everything you do that effects the organization's objectives and their well-being in your employees' eyes. The concentration of respected leaders is on what they are [be] such as character and beliefs, what they know such as human nature, tasks, and job, and what they do such as motivating, implementing, and providing direction.

Chapter

3

Types Of Leadership

CHAPTER 3 – TYPES OF LEADERSHIP

Authoritative leadership (Autocratic)

Authoritarian leaders, otherwise called autocratic leaders, give clear desire to what should be done, how it ought to be done, and when it ought to be done. There is additionally a reasonable division between the followers and the leader. Authoritarian leaders settle on choices with practically zero contributions from the rest of the group freely.

Researchers found that settling on choices was less creative. Lewin likewise found that under authoritarian leadership, it is harder to move from an authoritarian style to a democratic style than the other way around. Misuse of this style is normally seen as bossy, controlling, and dictatorial. Authoritarian leadership is best connected to circumstances where the leader is the most educated individual of the group or where there is little time for cooperative choice-making.

A leadership style portrayed by individual control over all choices and little contribution from group members is Autocratic Leadership, otherwise called authoritarian leadership. Autocratic leaders' taking into account their own particular thoughts and judgments settle on decisions and rarely make any acknowledge to their followers guidance. Autocratic leadership includes absolute, authoritarian control over a group.

Attributes of Autocratic Leadership

Some of the essential attributes of autocratic leadership include:

- Leaders settle on choices
- Little or no contribution from group members
- Group members are seldom trusted with choices or vital tasks
- Group leaders direct all the work techniques and procedures

Advantages of Autocratic Leadership

In a few examples, Autocratic leadership can be helpful for instance when without consulting with a large group of individuals choices should be made rapidly. A few activities in order to get things fulfilled rapidly and proficiently require solid leadership.

Have you ever worked with associates or a gathering of students on a project that got wrecked by absence of leadership, poor association, and failure to set due dates? Assuming this is the case; odds are that your task execution or evaluation endured subsequently. A solid leader in such circumstances, who uses an autocratic style can allot tasks to various individuals, assume responsibility of the group, and set up due dates which are solid for activities to be done.

In circumstances that are especially unpleasant, for example during military clashes, group members may really incline towards autocratic style. Individuals of the group are permitted to concentrate on performing particular tasks without stressing about settling on complex choices. This permits group members to likewise end up exceedingly talented at performing specific obligations, which can be valuable to the group.

Drawbacks of Autocratic Leadership

While now and again, autocratic leadership cans be gainful, there are additionally numerous occasions where this leadership style can be risky. Individuals who misuse an autocratic leadership style are frequently seen as dictatorial, and bossy, which can lead to hatred among group members.

Individuals in the group may disdain that they can't contribute thoughts since autocratic leaders settle on choices without consulting the group. Additionally, researchers have found that autocratic leadership can cause absence of innovative solutions to problems, which can at last hurt the performance of the group.

Leaders can figure out how to utilize components of this style wisely while autocratic leadership has some potential pitfalls. An autocratic style can, for instance, be utilized adequately in circumstances where the leader has access to data that other members of the group do not or is the most educated individual of the group.

Participative Leadership (Democratic)

Lewin's study found that participative leadership, otherwise called democratic leadership, is generally the best leadership style. Democratic leaders offer direction to group individuals, however, they permit contribution from other group individuals and likewise take part in the group. In Lewin's study, individuals in this group were more gainful than the individuals of the authoritarian group; their commitments were also of a much higher quality.

Group individuals are urged to take part by participative leaders; however, the leader holds the last say over the choice taking process. Group individuals are more roused and inventive and feel occupied in the procedure.

Democratic leadership, otherwise called participative leadership, is a type of leadership style in which individuals of the group play a more participative role in choice making procedures. This learning style is generally a stand out of the most effective and leads to higher profitability, better contributions from group individuals, and expanded group morale as found by Researchers.

Attributes of Democratic Leadership

Some of the essential attributes of democratic leadership include:

- Creativity is energized and remunerated

- Members of the group feel more occupied with procedures

- Despite the fact that the leader holds the final say over choices, group individuals are urged to impart thoughts and opinions

Advantages of Democratic Leadership

Democratic leadership can lead to better thoughts and more inventive solutions to problems since group individuals are urged to share their ideas. Group individuals additionally feel more included and resolved to projects, making them more prone to think about the final products. Research on leadership styles has likewise demonstrated that democratic leadership leads to higher profitability among group individuals.

Drawbacks of Democratic Leadership

Democratic leadership has some potential drawbacks while it has been depicted as the best leadership style; it, in circumstances where time is of the essence or parts are misty, democratic leadership can lead to correspondent disappointment and uncompleted tasks. Now and again, group individuals might not have the ability to settle on quality contributions to the choice making process or the information.

In circumstances where group individuals are gifted and anxious to share their insight, democratic leadership works best. It is likewise critical to build up an arrangement, have a lot of time to permit individuals to contribute, and after then vote on the best strategy.

Delegative (Laissez-Faire) Leadership

Individuals under delegative leadership, otherwise called laissez-fair leadership, as found by researchers, were the least profitable of all three groups. The individuals in this group made more requests likewise on the leader, were not able to work freely, and indicated little cooperation.

Delegative leaders offer to group individuals next to zero direction and leave decision-making up to group individuals. While this style can be in circumstances where group individuals are highly qualified in an area of expertise compelling, it frequently leads to absence of inspiration and inadequate roles.

Laissez-faire leadership, also known as delegative leadership, is a kind of leadership style in which leaders permits group individuals to settle on choices and is hands-off. Researchers have found that generally, this is the leadership style that leads to the least profitability among group individuals.

Attributes of Delegative Leadership

Laissez-faire leadership is described by:

- Complete flexibility for followers to decide

- Very little direction from leaders

- Group individuals are expected to take care of problems on their own

- Leaders gives the tools and resources required

Laissez-faire leadership can be effective in circumstances where group individuals are highly talented, motivated and have the ability of working on their own. While the ordinary term for this style is 'laissez-faire' and suggests a methodology of total hands-off, numerous leaders still stay accessible and open to group individuals for criticism and counsel.

Drawbacks of Laissez-Faire Leadership

Laissez-faire leadership in circumstances where group individuals do not have the experience or learning required to finish tasks and make choices is not perfect. A few people are not good at dealing with their own task, setting their own due dates and taking care of issues all alone. Projects can go off-track and due dates can be missed when colleagues do not get enough direction or feedback from leaders in such circumstances.

Chapter

4

Leaders/Managers

Chapter 4 – Leaders/Managers

Toward a distinction between leadership vs. management, the trend in today's business culture is progressing rapidly, and those who are being led rather than managed are showing signs of higher productivity, increased job satisfaction as well as a higher potential than ever before. Depending on both your employment history and your management style, the paradigm shift that must take place in this transition to leading from managing can be quite substantial.

Than someone who is by nature an open team- player who enjoys participation with others more than achieving standards, you may have more difficulty making the shift if you're an authoritative type who functions best when there are lots of standards and rules and everyone is being managed to adhere to those standards. The trend toward leadership is growing, whatever your natural style, and encouraging is the result of teams operating in this way. Let's have a look at the difference between a leader and a manager.

Managers

Because managers are working in a hierarchy they manage, a manager by definition, has a higher position than those who work for him/her, and who are called subordinates. Typically, they have power over another group of people, evaluate their performance and make decisions about how those people will work. Within a hierarchical structure, it is a formal authority. The subordinates do what they are told to do and their salary is often the primary motivator for their performance. Typically, managers are also subordinates to someone else, and using their subordinate workforce to get a job done, they are paid.

To the manager, since the performance of the workforce reflects on their management performance, this translates into productivity being of primary importance. Managers according to recent research, tend to be people who lead relatively comfortable lives and have come from stable backgrounds. They tend not to be risk-takers. It is important in a hierarchical workforce that the team looks upon the manager as less prone to making mistakes and more knowledgeable than they are.

Leaders

By contrast, leaders, do not have subordinates, they choose to give up their formal authority and invite people to follow, even if they are working in hierarchical organizations. Leaders tend to be more people-focused than task-focused they tend to have a more charismatic style and understand that telling people what to do does not necessarily inspire them to follow you. Leaders are always interested in seeing development and growth in those they are leading.

This does not mean a leader cannot be task-focused - many are, in fact, but they know how to motivate others to work toward common goals and visions and encourage loyalty. Leaders are comfortable with making changes when problems come along. They appear to be much more likely to take risks and are not afraid for the betterment of the team, of confrontation and conflict. Leaders use their mistakes as learning tools for the team, and willingly admit them.

Because studies show people are less motivated by money and highly motivated by job satisfaction, the feeling of doing meaningful work and making a difference that is valued by others, the trend of making a transition to leadership from management is occurring. In general, people prefer to be led rather than managed. In our culture, traditional management still functions and works. A leadership style of management however produces greater results. Author and Leadership expert Jim Clemmer says, "Leadership is a verb, not a noun. It is an action, not a position. It is what we do, not the role we are in."

In your business, if you have the freedom to make the visionary and behavioral transition to leading your employees from managing them, to see the difference it could make, it may be well worth the effort. You can adopt a leadership philosophy within your management style even if you are working within a company structure. With those you manage how can you make this transition? Here are some suggestions:

- Work alongside them on tasks and projects Rather than above them. Let them know you are interested in working with them more than just managing them.

- Anatmosphere conducive to teamwork should be provided. Create for staff opportunities to contribute their thoughts and ideas about what's happening in the business.

- Invite the input of   those you work with. This does not mean you are bound to accept every piece of advice or suggestion given to you, but you will inspire them if you truly consider every person's input and value their willingness to give it to you.

- Rather than telling them what they need to do, inspire them to work with you. When people feel valued, satisfied and significant in their work, they are more productive, more creative, more willing to put in extra time and effort.

- From your   workplace, remove hierarchical language. Language is a powerful thing, and it can influence how others view you and the way people view themselves. Rather than people who work for you, begin introducing co-workers as people you work with.

- For strengthening your team, provide teamwork training. When individuals reach their goals or deliver exceptional performance, acknowledge their successes.

- When one person is struggling beneath a heavy workload, pass it on – this fosters a shared sense of teamwork and purpose within the company. Share the load.

- Be vulnerable with your team. Let them know where your weaknesses are, and where you struggle. You will be respected for your authenticity and be more motivated to put their shoulders to the wheel and help out when you need it.

The transition to leading from managing can produce great results. To see how your team responds, try making a few changes. You will find your team working faster, harder and better than ever before if you get the results that are typical with this kind of transition.

Chapter

5

Leadership In Business

CHAPTER 5 – LEADERSHIP IN BUSINESS

Seeing the connection between business and external trends, encouraging innovation and framing challenges that inspire it, creating the conditions to enable leadership to emerge throughout the business, utilizing language and symbols efficiently, influencing mindsets and culture, creating appropriate metrics, and recognizing and rewarding positive outcomes and new behaviors are all roles of the emerging business leader. In the face of vested interests, many leaders who were interviewed for a study had spoke of the importance of courage in raising difficult issues and making sure that followers have support in the places they need it.

A new leadership role has been leading change past business limits. A number of the interviewees also identified a critical change in the scope of their work. More and more they now see it as their role to lead beyond the conventional boundaries of their organization, proactively driving change in consumer and supplier behavior, industry norms and government policy, for the common advantage of their organizations and larger society. Some are leading collaboratively with industry competitors, NGOs and government organizations where challenges need to be tackled and only collective, systemic solutions will do.

This new horizon to their part has obliged leaders to develop skill in areas that historically have not been a conventional part of the business leader's repertoire: with an informed point of view contributing to public debate, proactively leading change in supplier and consumer behavior, industry norms and government policy, relating well with multiple constituencies, engaging in dialogue to comprehend and empathize with communities with perspectives contrary to one's own, and engaging in multi-stakeholder collaboration with unconventional partners.

Anticipate

At detecting ambiguous threats and opportunities on the periphery of their business, most organizations and leaders are poor. Famously, Coors executives were late seeing the trend toward low carbohydrate beers.

In toys and gaming, Lego management missed the electronic revolution. In contrast, strategic leaders are constantly vigilant by scanning the environment for signals of change and honing their ability to anticipate. I worked with a CEO named Mike once, who in heavy manufacturing businesses had built his reputation as a turn-around wizard. He was terrific at reacting to fixing systems and crises. Mike's company enjoyed a bump in growth, fueled in part by an up cycle, after he'd worked his magic in one particular crisis. But demand abruptly softened after the cycle had peaked, catching Mike off guard.

More of the same wasn't going to work in a down market. Mike needed to gather better information from diverse sources in order to anticipate where his industry was headed and consider various scenarios. From both inside and outside the organization, I showed Mike and his team members how to pick up weak signals. They worked to take the perspective of customers, competitors, and partners and to develop broader networks. Mike and the team diversified their product portfolio and acquired a company in an adjacent market where demand was higher and less susceptible to boom-and-bust cycles, more alert to opportunities outside the core business.

To improve your ability to anticipate: Talk to your suppliers, customers, and other partners to understand their challenges. Conduct market research and business simulations to understand competitors' perspectives, gauge their likely reactions to new initiatives or products, and predict potential disruptive offerings. To imagine various futures and prepare for the unexpected, use scenario planning. Look at a fast-growing rival and examine actions it has taken that puzzle you. List recent customers you have lost and try to figure out why. In other industries or functions, attend conferences and events.

Challenge

The status quo is being questioned by Strategic thinkers. They encourage divergent points of view and challenge their own and others' assumptions. They do take decisive action, only after careful reflection and examination of a problem through many lenses. This requires courage, patience, and an open mind. Consider Chandler, a division president in an energy company that I once worked with, who was set in his ways and avoided risky or messy situations. He would gather all available information and retreat alone into his office when faced with a tough problem—for example, how to consolidate business units to streamline costs.

His solutions, although very well thought out, were rarely innovative and predictable. He focused entirely on two similar and underperforming businesses instead of considering a bolder reorganization that would streamline activities over the whole division in the consolidation case. When he needed outside advice he turned to a few seasoned consultants in one trusted firm who suggested tried-and-true solutions instead of questioning basic industry assumptions.

I helped Chandler learn how to invite different (even opposing) views to challenge his own thinking and that of his advisers through coaching. At first, this was uncomfortable for him, but then, he began to see that he could improve his strategic decision making and generate fresh solutions to stale problems. He even assigned a colleague to play devil's advocate for the organizational streamlining, an approach that yielded a hybrid solution.

Focus on the root causes of a problem rather than the symptoms, to improve your ability to challenge, apply the "five whys" of Sakichi Toyoda, Toyota's founder. ("product returns increased 5% this month." "Why?" "Because the product intermittently malfunctions." "Why?" and so on.) List longstanding assumptions about an aspect of your business ("Our customers are prevented from defecting by the high switching costs") and inquire of a diverse group if they hold true.

Encourage debate by holding "safe zone" meetings where open dialogue and conflict are expected and welcomed. Create a rotating position for the express purpose of questioning the status quo. To surface challenges early, include naysayers in a decision process. Capture input from people not directly affected by a decision who may have a good perspective on the repercussions.

Interpret

Invariably, leaders who challenge in the right way elicit conflicting and complex information. That's why the best ones are also able to interpret. You should synthesize all the input you have, instead of reflexively seeing or hearing what you expect. You'll need to recognize patterns, push through ambiguity, and seek new insights. J.K. Paasikivi, Finland's former president was fond of saying that wisdom begins by recognizing the facts and then "recognizing," or rethinking them to expose their hidden implications. Liz, a U.S. food company CMO, was developing a marketing plan for the company's low carbohydrate cake line some years ago.

The Atkins diet was popular at the time, and every food company had a low carbohydrate strategy. But Liz noticed that none of the buyers she listened to were keeping away from the company's snacks because they were on a low carbohydrate diet. Rather, because they contained sugar, a fast-growing segment people with diabetes shunned them. Liz thought if it began to serve diabetics rather than fickle dieters, her company might achieve higher sales. Her ability to connect the dots ultimately led to a profitable change in product mix from low carbohydrate to sugar-free cakes.

List at least three possible explanations for what you're observing and invite perspectives from diverse stakeholders to improve your ability to interpret. When analyzing ambiguous data, force yourself to zoom in on the details and out to see the big picture. Look for missing information and evidence that disconfirms your hypothesis actively. Supplement observation with quantitative analysis. Step away, go for a walk, look at art, put on nontraditional music, or even play Ping-Pong to promote an open mind.

Decide

Decision makers may have to make tough calls with incomplete information, and often they must do so quickly in uncertain times. But at the outset, strategic thinkers insist on multiple options and don't get prematurely locked into simplistic go/no-go choices. They don't shoot from the hip but follow a disciplined process that balances rigor with speed, considers the trade-offs involved, and considers both short-term and long-term goals. Strategic leaders must have the courage of their convictions informed by a robust decision process in the end. An execution-oriented division president in a technology business, Janeece, liked to make decisions quickly and keep the process simple.

When the competitive landscape was familiar and the choices straightforward, this worked well. Unfortunately for her, as nontraditional competitors from Korea began seizing market share with lower-priced products, the industry was shifting rapidly. Janeece's instinct was to make a strategic acquisition in a low-cost geography, which was a yes or no proposition, to preserve the company's competitive pricing position and market share.

She pushed for a rapid green light as the plan's champion, but the CEO and the CFO resisted because capital was short. Surprised by this, she gathered the principals involved in the decision and challenged them to come up with other options. The team elected to explore the possibility of a joint venture or a strategic alliance and take a methodical approach. Janeece ultimately pursued an acquisition but of a different company in a more strategic market on the basis of that analysis.

Reframe binary decisions by explicitly asking your team to improve your capacity to decide, "What different options do we have?" Partition big decisions into pieces to understand component parts and better see unintended consequences. Tailor your decision criteria to long-term versus short-term projects. In your decision process, let others know where you are. Are you still seeking divergent ideas and debate, or are you moving toward closure and choice? Determine who can influence the success of your decision and who needs to be directly involved. Instead of big bets, consider pilots or experiments and make staged commitments.

Align

At finding common ground and achieving buy-in among stakeholders who have disparate views and agendas, strategic leaders must be adept. This requires active outreach. Success depends on proactive communication, frequent engagement, and trust building. An executive that I worked with, a chemical company president in charge of the Chinese market was tireless in trying to expand his business. But he had difficulty getting support from colleagues elsewhere in the world. He plowed forward alone, frustrated that they didn't share his enthusiasm for opportunities in China, further alienating them.

A survey revealed that his partners didn't completely comprehend his strategy and thus hesitated to back him. The president turned the situation around with my help. He began to have consistent face-to-face meetings with his fellow leaders in which he detailed his development plans and solicited feedback, participation, and differing points of view. Gradually they began to see the benefits for their own functions and lines of business. With more noteworthy collaboration, sales increased, and rather than obstacles, the president came to see his colleagues as strategic partners.

Communicate early and often to combat the two most common complaints in organizations:

To improve your ability to align:

"No one ever told me" and "no one ever asked me."

Identify vital internal and external stakeholders, mapping their stands on your initiative and pinpointing any misalignment of interests. Look for hidden agendas and coalitions. Use facilitated conversations and structure to expose areas of resistance or misunderstanding. Reach out directly to resisters to understand their concerns and then address them. During the rollout of your initiative or strategy, be vigilant in monitoring stakeholders' positions. Recognize and otherwise reward colleagues who support team alignment.

Learn

For organizational learning, strategic leaders are the focal point. They search for the lessons in both successful and unsuccessful outcomes, and they promote a culture of inquiry. In an open, constructive way to find the hidden lessons, they study failures of their own and of their teams'. Including the CEO, a team of 40 senior leaders from a pharmaceutical company, took a Strategic Aptitude Self-Assessment and discovered that their weakest collective area of leadership was learning. It emerged, at all levels of the company, that the tendency was to punish instead of learn from mistakes, which implied that leaders often went to great lengths to cover up their own.

The CEO realized that if the company was to become more innovative then the culture had to change. The team launched three initiatives under his leadership:

(1) An innovation tournament to generate new ideas from across the organization. Meanwhile, the CEO himself became more open in acknowledging his missteps.

(2) A program to publicize stories about projects that initially failed but ultimately led to creative solutions.

(3) A program to engage cross-divisional groups in novel experiments to take care of client issues and then report the results regardless of outcome.

For instance, he described to a group of high potentials how his delay in selling a slowed down legacy business unit had kept the enterprise from acquiring a diagnostics company that would have expanded its market share. The lesson, he explained, was that on underperforming investments, he should more readily cut losses. In time the company culture shifted toward more shared learning and bolder innovation.

Family leadership

Family members and parents within their own families become natural leaders. In many different aspects of life, they advocate for their own child's education, childcare, medical care, and much more. Many parents eventually feel the desire to "reach back" and help other families, and try to change systems and services to better serve all children.

Some of the key values, skills, and competency sets that provide a foundation for all family leaders, whether they are advocating for their own family's needs, supporting other families, or trying to change policies and systems, to make positive change for children and families are listed below, yet, these do apply to all leaders.

A family leader:

- Accepts that each person has strengths and weaknesses
- Views all people as valuable regardless of their abilities
- Shows concern for others
- Believes anyone can learn and improve
- Listens to others and asks for their perspective
- Identifies the needs and feelings of others
- Shares personal experiences openly
- Respects others and doesn't judge

- Embraces own strengths and weaknesses

- Expresses self clearly to others

- Accepts risks and outcomes of decisions made

- Advocates for what the family needs

- Maintains a positive attitude about professionals encountered while accessing services

- Makes decisions and solves problems for family unit

- Works with minimal praise or recognition

- Participates in and monitors the services provided for own family

The list of values and skills of competencies and skill sets above should not be considered "prerequisites" but rather as they strive to become more family driven, a guide for family organizations, leaders, and policymakers. This is to say that as family leaders participate in opportunities at all levels they develop and enhance skills. Systems and organizations should not hesitate to recruit and utilize family leaders who may not have all the competencies and characteristics reflected in this guide yet perceive that they should provide opportunities for family leaders to continue to develop new skills.

Community Leadership

Without effective local government, we have established that central government cannot address key priorities. Creating sustainable communities, places where people want to work and live – now and in the future – for local government to push beyond their traditional service delivery role and their role as community leaders, requires a new responsibility.

At NLGN's Policy Summit, the discussion produced the following ideas about why local authorities are well positioned to play this role, what tools they might need to carry out the role, and what community leadership will mean to them in terms of both the impact on their functions and responsibilities.

The conditions community leadership role of local government is founded on its democratic legitimacy and responsibility as the primary locally elected body. All things considered, local government has a mandate to represent and act on behalf of the whole community, and to think across service boundaries and silos. Also local authorities have a unique 'sense of place', of a distinct geographical area, as a local level body. They were put in a unique position with regard to local communities by these roots in the locality.

Local authorities have an over-arching representative role in an area which no other body can provide, representing local communities. Councils can use this representative function to articulate the views of, and lead, the local community in performing a community leadership role. This involves listening to the local community, ascertaining what they want and brokering between the different views.

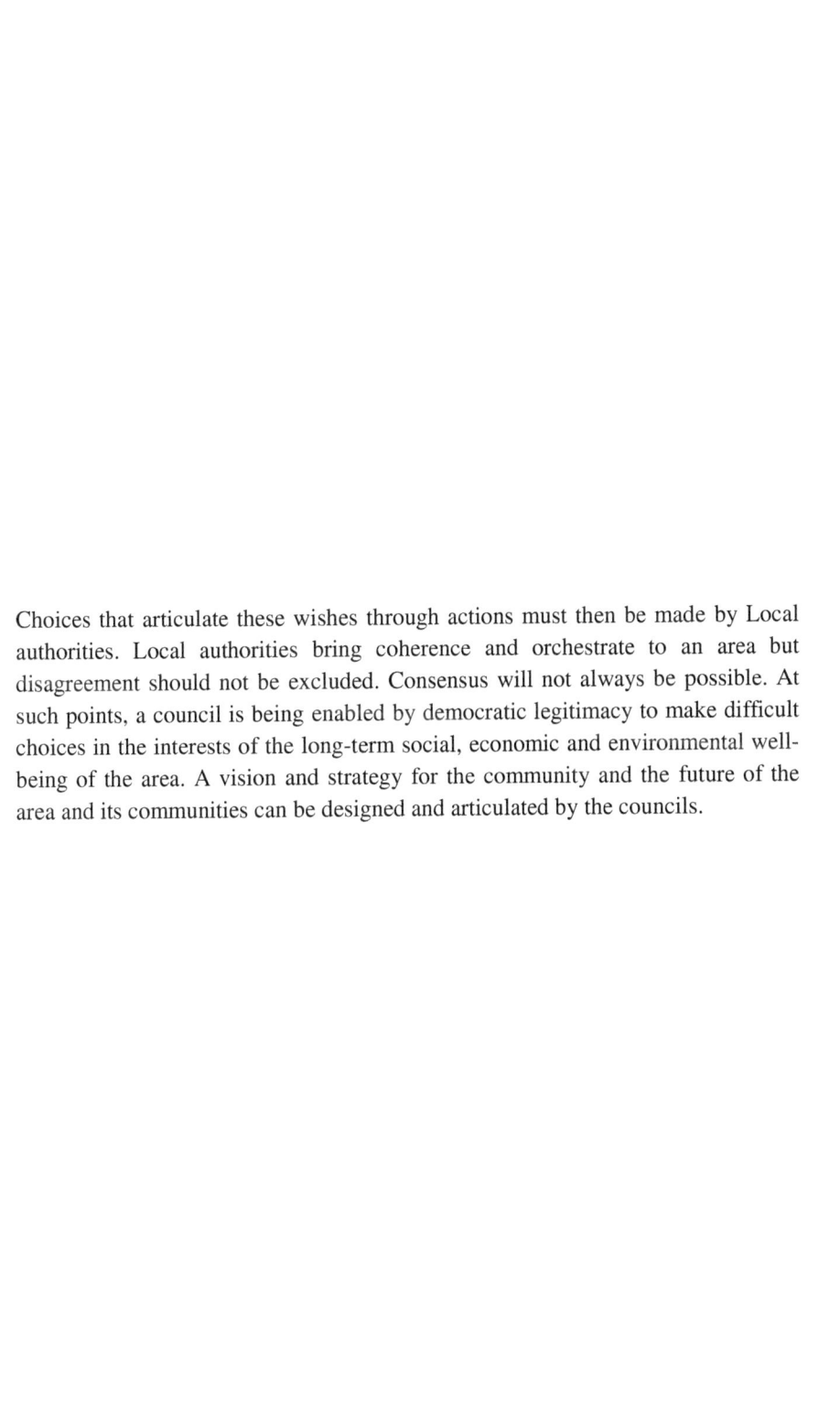

Choices that articulate these wishes through actions must then be made by Local authorities. Local authorities bring coherence and orchestrate to an area but disagreement should not be excluded. Consensus will not always be possible. At such points, a council is being enabled by democratic legitimacy to make difficult choices in the interests of the long-term social, economic and environmental well-being of the area. A vision and strategy for the community and the future of the area and its communities can be designed and articulated by the councils.

At different levels, councilors have a key role to play in community leadership. An essential local knowledge is provided by them, usually living in the areas they represent (unlike many officers). Strong and close local relationships must be built by them; at higher levels, ensuring local needs are represented. Community leadership is about political leadership as well as managerial competency.

Local government can assume an essential role in engaging local people in the political process, engaging communities by performing a representative role through listening and articulating citizens' views. Community leadership is about creating opportunities to render greater community empowerment, creating trust at the local level and galvanizing people.

Essentially, creation of community architecture should be involved by the council's community leadership role, through which a dialogue with their elected representative's citizens can be involved in decision-making, exercising their influence and articulating what they want, possibly through very local structures such as neighborhood governance or area committees.

Local government has the potential to help build social capital by creating a situation where people have a voice and stake in improvement of their local areas, building social capital through engaging with and empowering citizens and communities, and where they feel that if they want to influence something then they are able to do so.

Whilst most agree that councils need to continue to deliver at least some services in order to maintain legitimacy and credibility, to create the space and capacity to perform the developing community leadership role, it is also recognized that there must be a shift from emphasis on direct service delivery.

Councils are uniquely placed to play the important role of ensuring that services are delivered to a high standard, by uniting local partners, holding them to account and ensuring that services in a locality are joined-up, however, whilst not necessarily providing or even purchasing the services. Accountability for services in a locality ultimately lies at local government's door as a body with over-arching legitimacy. It is to the council that citizens turn when something goes wrong in the police or health services. People do need a route of accountability when they are dissatisfied with services and that is where elected representatives can play an important role – promoting good practice and mediating when things go wrong – as a lynchpin in the system.

A fundamental facet of the community leadership role must therefore be the capacity to influence local partners and agencies and act to solve problems that arise, influencing a wider set of services. This role demands that councils extend their reach to influence issues and organizations beyond their direct sphere of control and responsibility. Councils can further build their legitimacy and ownership within the community in extending beyond their core services and networking, influencing, persuading people.

Local partners do recognize that the local authority has a special role within a locality that derives from their representative role. In terms of ensuring a high standard of service delivery, partners realize that real leadership from the local authority can be a great advantage. They also recognize that with the council, it is important to have a good working relationship.

Community Leadership: What does it look like?

Described above are many features of community leadership, all of which beyond core service delivery within a locality refer to the 'extra'. Also, for a study, leaders were asked for direct and tangible examples of what community leadership within individual localities might mean, of which some examples are listed below. However, core to this discussion was an agreement that under a banner of 'Community Leadership' the activities conducted to some extent will differ for each locality, reflecting local circumstance and needs.

Examples included:

• Deciding, because of concerns about alcohol misuse or disorder, not to license a new local casino and the wider impact this might have on the environmental and social well-being of the area.

 • Using, in response to permanent closures of the latter, rural mobile libraries as Post Offices.

• Freeing up land owned by the council for development by others in tune with local plans and vision.

• Funding, in order to improve local livability, the cleaning up of space or land owned by other organizations.

• Providing, in the event of an international disaster, a point of contact.

• For a likely change in the local economy, long term planning – for example, closure of a dominant local industry and the impact that this will have on local employment.

Chapter

6

Attributes Or 'Personality Traits' Of Good Leaders

CHAPTER 6 – ATTRIBUTES OR 'PERSONALITY TRAITS' OF GOOD LEADERS

Vigorous & Enthusiastic:

Some individuals can drain the life out of you; they are similar to energy vampires. Where compelling leaders are concerned it's different. They do the inverse and make you feel empowered and connected truly basically by their excited and perky natures. There is real passion for what they do in them.

Charming:

In (1968), charisma was depicted by Weber as "a certain quality of an individual personality by virtue of which he is set apart from ordinary men and treated as endowed with supernatural, superhuman, or at least specifically exceptional qualities."

Others can be moved by charisma in the way that it offers articulation of confidence in follower's abilities to accomplish exclusive expectations. The First Impression Can Seal the Deal!

Open:

The life blood of a compelling administration is the eagerness to communicate straightforward. The best leaders have confidence in openness and they want to speak to individuals in their group. Added to this, they have other individual qualities, such as mindfulness and self-control which help them communicate successfully.

Self-Motivated:

First off, the bar is constantly set higher by the best leaders regarding their own particular execution. They are self-inspired and never settle for second best and are objective- orientated people; they expect others to do the same as well. All things considered, they are reasonable by the way they request from the people around them that additional effort be put into everything they do.

Committed:

Dreamers are separated from doers by their level of commitment. It is to the soldier, going over the slope, not realizing what's waiting on the opposite side. It is to the boxer getting off the mat once again after having been thumped down. It is to the marathon runner, pushing another ten miles even after their strength is no more. It is to the leader, all that and more in light of the fact that everyone you lead is relying upon you.

Future-Oriented:

Effective leaders never allow people who keep away from troublesome issues, or 'headless chickens', to sit while going back and forth or switching positions constantly to suit whichever way the wind is blowing. The best leaders have a clear idea of where they want the business to go and those perspectives are formed with a touch of intuition tossed in for good measure in light of strong proof. They issue the vision out and adjust it if need be with their senior individual until they feel certain it is the most ideal way to go when the vision is clear. At that point, they can win support all through the department, or business, for that vision and can later make an interpretation and turn those wide yearnings into significant objectives, methodology and arrangement which serve to connect individuals and aide their activities.

Intelligent:

The best leaders are savvy characters, not always book smart; however instead, they are people who benefit from having distinctive forms of insight: the ability to investigate and tackle issues, learning identified with the prerequisites of their job or a capacity to be inventive. They additionally dependably appear to have an aiding of that basic, if to some degree immaterial, item named common sense. They settle on choices just when they have all the information at hand, in light of the fact they involve others in the decision-making procedures, and they benefit from their intelligence and experience.

Purpose driven:

Great leaders are purpose-driven. Not only do they comprehend what to do, they know why they are doing it. They're likewise able to help other people tap into the power of why. What level of purpose do you have now? What capacity would you be able to grow to, becoming a more effective leader? Ask yourself how you would depict what you do for a living? Is it work? Your profession? Or is it your main goal? Work tends to take more than it gives you. A career might be something you anticipate and put some vitality into. In any case, on the off chance it's your mission, it is a powerful source of mental and spiritual energy.

Open to Change:

The best leaders are individuals who are not hesitant to attempt diverse things. New is great, as far as they are concerned, on the off chance that it means possibly accomplishing better results. Now, the best leaders with regards to finding new routes forward, do not as a matter of course imagine that no one but they can spot essential patterns and changes or that they have all the winning thoughts. No, in such manner what distinguishes them is that, first, they are interested in change. They embrace it in fact. Secondly, they make an environment where recommendations and thoughts are invited from numerous sources so throughout the business the stream of inventiveness is encouraged.

Inclusive:

Nowadays, a lot of directors discuss inclusivity but the truth where some are concerned, does not generally coordinate the words. Seeing as viable leaders are open and confident characters with genuine sympathy for others, they like to engage individuals, of course where appropriate, in the running of the business. They are never afraid to loosen the reins or delegate to others, if they believe that will deliver the best results. For sure, like all human beings, they prefer some people over others, but they treat all fairly and never take dislikes to people for no reason, nor do they allow cliques to form amongst their employees. They really do think in terms of teams. Everyone has a chance to participate and contribute.

Focus:

The sharper the focus, the sharper you are. The keys are priorities and concentration. A leader who knows what his priorities are but lacks concentration knows what to do but never gets it done. If he has concentration but no priorities, he has excellence without progress. But when he harnesses both, he has the potential to achieve great things.

Learn from mistakes:

Of course, even the very best leaders are not immune from making mistakes. Sometimes you see top leaders being portrayed as infallible messiahs who never make a wrong step. That's wishful thinking. Sure, the best leaders make fewer mistakes than others do, but that's largely due to the effective decision-making processes they follow in the first place. When things do go awry, top leaders see those events as learning opportunities and move on. They do not make the same mistake twice.

Ethical:

There have been many examples of business, and indeed other leaders, who have spectacularly fallen from grace in recent times, and yes, they all fell for different reasons, but a big factor in all their downfalls was that they each lost their moral compass – or maybe they never had one in the first place. In some cases not having such a compass can lead to greed taking precedence over ethics, or in other words 'self' starts to matter most. Lots of things go wrong when you lose sight of your ethics and it always leads to negative outcomes in the long run. The best leaders in any business, though, do have a moral compass and more importantly, they follow it.

Self-Control:

This is another important trait that all the best leaders possess. It's vital because it helps them in so many aspects of leading and managing others. For starters, it allows them to think clearly, which helps in decision-making and that in turn results in fewer mistakes. It also helps them to act rationally, not emotionally, when faced with difficult people, so they can decide which leadership style is best to apply in any given situation.

Adversity Quotient and Leaders

Stoltz and his group in a recent doctoral paper, thought about the adversity quotients of business leaders and educational leaders. In one discovery there are indications that normal educational leaders had brought down adversity quotients essentially. It is important to note that adversity quotient is not prone or situational to be changed without appropriate mindfulness and training to fortify one's core and response abilities over the course of one's existence.

As indicated by Stoltz, one clarification is that this outcome may come from these people's original professional choices. Individuals who have a tendency to choose professions where they see more prominent opportunity and less adversity are those with lower AQs, they naturally realize that they are less prepared for adversity-rich careers. Those with higher adversity quotient in any case, don't as a matter of course pick more difficult lives. Numerous high AQ individuals like to go into education since they want to have an intentional and compensating career.

Stoltz and his group on the light of their analysis of turnover found that numerous sensibly high AQ individuals found that it is so hard to execute change in a bureaucratic environment. So some individuals moved to other professions, possibly reducing the overall adversity quotient mean among those who remain. In one case, lower adversity quotient individuals may have sensed that their operating systems could not handle the same capacity as those with higher adversity quotients. As a result, they sought jobs that they believed would be less demanding only to find out that education is rich in adversity.

In another case, the educational establishment was seen as an overhang, nudging the higher adversity quotient individuals to seek other ways to live. Adversity quotients can fundamentally influence one's career choice, regardless of industry, passion for one's work, the difficulty one is willing to take on, and one's patience with inertia.

Chapter

7

Steps To Great Leadership

CHAPTER 7 – STEPS TO GREAT LEADERSHIP

Leadership skills are the devices, practices, and capabilities that a person needs in order to be effective at motivating and coordinating others. The following are guides to achieving great leadership skills.

Understand yourself

You must have an understanding of your identity as a leader, what you can do and what you know. Seeking self-change implies constantly reinforcing your traits. This can be accomplished through formal classes, self-study, reflection, and communicating with others. Take note that it's not the leader or another person but the followers who figure out whether the leader is fruitful. On the off chance that they do not lack confidence or trust in their leader, then they will be unmotivated. To be fruitful you have to persuade not yourself or your superiors but your followers that you are worthy of emulation.

Understand your followers

Become acquainted with the people around you. Everyone has distinctive capacities, wants, needs, and purpose in life. To coexist with others and get results, you need to get to know them.

- The only way to get to know someone is through direct individual contact. Interact with group individuals as frequently as possible.

- Observe every individual's unique qualities and attributes. Become acquainted with each individual from your group.

Different individuals require distinct styles of leadership. Another contract for instance, requires more supervision than an expertise employee does. An individual who lacks motivation requires an alternate methodology than one with a high level of inspiration. You must know your people! The basic beginning stage is having a decent comprehension of human instinct, for example needs, inspiration, and feelings. You should come to know your followers' be, know, and do characteristics.

Understand the Situation

All situations are different. You must use your judgment to decide the best course of action and the leadership style needed for each situation. What you do in one situation will not always work in another. You may need to, for example, confront an employee for inappropriate behavior, but if the confrontation is too harsh or too weak, too late or too early, then the results may prove ineffective.

Problem solve in a step-by-step way whether you are faced with a decision to make or a conflict to resolve. Following a logical approach will help.

- State the problem as unmistakably and basically as possible.

- Gather all available resources and pertinent information.

- Brainstorm the greatest numbers of solutions or ideas as you can think of (with others if possible).

- Evaluate every solution or thought and choose the best one.

- Design an arrangement for utilizing your solution or thoughts. Incorporate a timetable, resources, and assigned roles to be utilized.

- Follow up on your plan by asking if your thought worked and why or why not.

Communication

You lead through two-way correspondence. A lot of it is nonverbal. For example, when you "set the case," that communicates that you would not request that they perform anything that you would not be willing to do to your people. What and how you get across either builds or destroys the relationship among you and your followers.

Communicate effectively – Effective communication is exchange. Obstructions are made by asking closed questions that evoke yes or no answers, talking down to individuals, utilizing intemperate authority, and advancing a society that relies upon unanimity. You'll create fear of openness and hinder the organization's development in the event that you center on winning the contention or if you react protectively to feedback.

Try these steps to effective communication:

- Listen and actively ask open ended questions. Be really intrigued by what others say.

- Point to areas of assertion before hopping on areas of contradiction as this lessens defensiveness; members won't fear being "assaulted."

- Set aside your power to make an atmosphere of partnership to reduce fear in group individuals.

- Thank people for their openness and emphasize how much you value it even if you don't like specifically what is being said.

- Portray contradiction as basically a difference of thoughts. Dispose of the "I'm correct, you're wrong" attitude.

- Promote a society of constructive dissent, though not to the point of paralysis.

Encourage enthusiasm and a sense of belonging

Show:

- **Integrity:** Members will consider assignments more important if you show that you're more intrigued by group objectives rather than your own personal benefits.

- **Understanding:** Everybody commits error. Attempt to be constructive, tolerant and thoughtful when offering feedback.

- **Fairness:** Equal treatment and equal opportunity lead to an equally good effort from all group individuals.

- **Friendliness:** Others will be more ready to share thoughts if you're interested in them as individuals too.

Keep everyone working toward agreed upon objectives

- Involve everyone in talks and decisions, even if asking for opinions and ideas implies an extended time of discussion.

- Harmonize contrasts and contradictions between group individuals by emphasizing compromise and cooperation.

- Remind everyone of the group's motivations occasionally. It's easy to become too narrowly focused and lose sight of the bigger goals.

- Provide consolation and inspiration, by showing your gratefulness for smart thoughts and extra effort.

Treat others as individuals. Put your knowledge and understanding of each group member to work!

- **Be imaginative.** A dull routine can bring about fatigue. An effective leader considers new and better approaches to old methods of doing things.

- **Be aware of expectations.** Everyone expects something different: acknowledgment, an opportunity to learn, a chance to work with other individuals and so on.

- **Delegate duties.** On the off chance that everybody shares the work, everybody can share pride in the group's achievements. Let each member know what's expected of him/her, available resources, due dates and so on.

- **Provide rewards.** Acknowledgment by the group is a well spring of individual fulfillment and positive reinforcement for a job well done.

Accept responsibility for getting things done

- **Seek help and information.** Ask for advice if you need it. This will encourage group involvement and help achieve group goals.

- **Take the initiative.** Why stand around and sit tight for another person to get things started? Set an example.

- **Offer help and information.** Your unique knowledge and skills might be exactly what's required.

- **Know when and how to say "no."** If your time and resources are already committed, turn down extra tasks, but do it pleasantly.

- **Make things happen.** By being decisive, vivacious, and excited, you can and will help complete tasks!

Master your emotions

Extraordinary leaders bring into uncertain environments certainty. That means you do have the inner conviction that you can find the answer and move forward. This doesn't mean that you have all the answers.

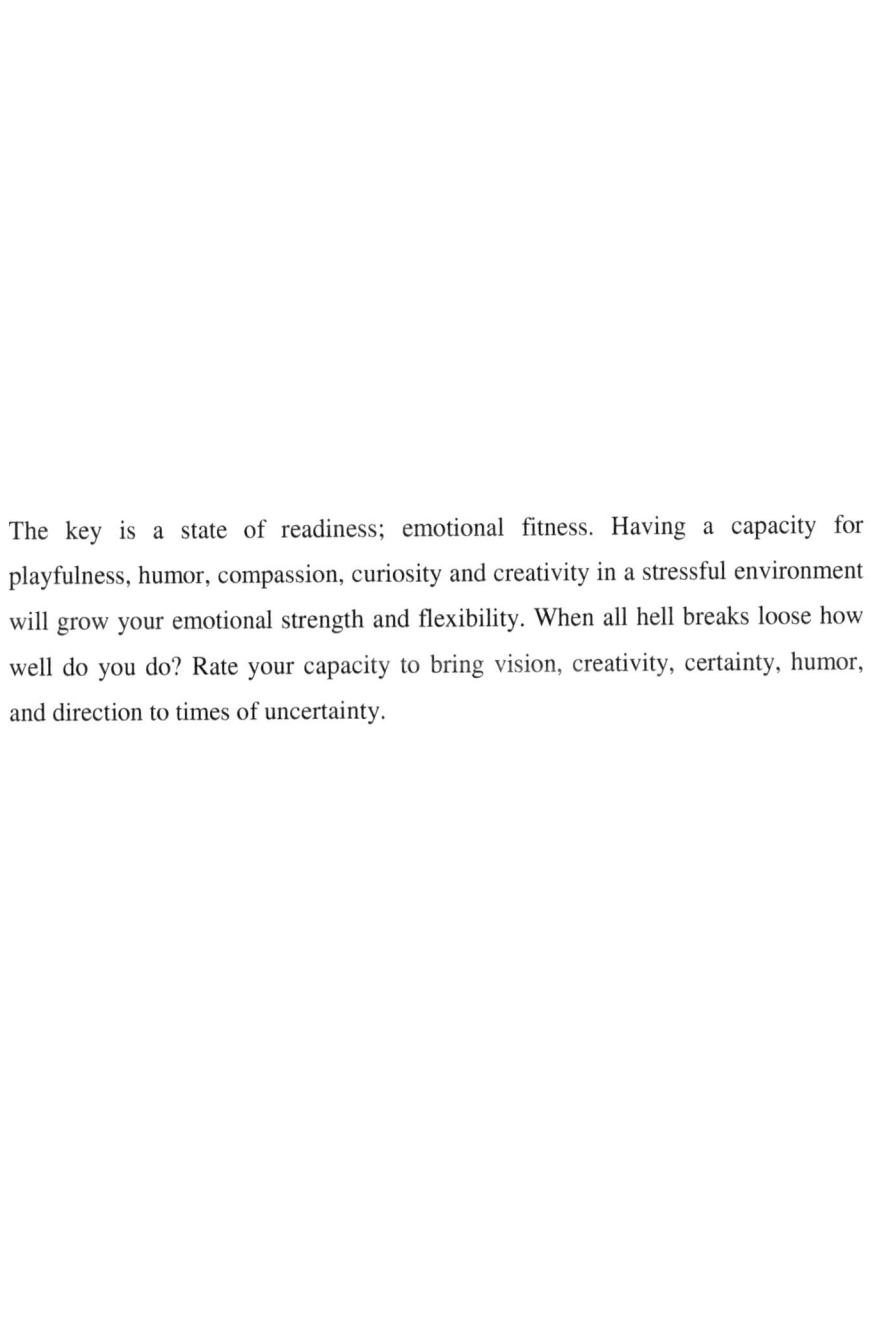

The key is a state of readiness; emotional fitness. Having a capacity for playfulness, humor, compassion, curiosity and creativity in a stressful environment will grow your emotional strength and flexibility. When all hell breaks loose how well do you do? Rate your capacity to bring vision, creativity, certainty, humor, and direction to times of uncertainty.

Chapter

8

Six Common Challenges Leaders Face Across Seven Countries

CHAPTER 8 – SIX COMMON CHALLENGES LEADERS FACE ACROSS SEVEN COUNTRIES

There are six main categories that comprise more than half of all challenges looking across the countries. These six, in addition, are ranked among the Top 10 challenges leaders face in each country. They are in order of frequency:

• **Developing Managerial Effectiveness:** The challenge of developing the relevant skills such as prioritization, time management, decision-making, strategic thinking, and getting up to speed with the job to be more effective at work.

• **Inspiring Others:** The challenge of motivating or inspiring others to ensure they are satisfied with their jobs; how to motivate a workforce to work smarter.

- **Developing Employees:** The challenge of developing others, including topics around coaching and mentoring.

- **Leading a Team:** The challenge of team management, team development, and team-building; how to support a team or instill pride in the team, what to do when taking over a new team, and how to lead a big team.

- **Guiding Change:** The challenge of understanding, managing, leading, and mobilizing change. How to overcome resistance to change, mitigate change consequences, and deal with employees' reaction to change.

- **Managing Politics and Internal Stakeholders:** The challenge of managing image, politics, and relationships. Gaining managerial support and managing up; getting buy-in from other individuals, departments, or groups.

CONCLUSION

In conclusion, being a leader involves making decisions that impact the lives of the followers. It is complicated and hard. Making sound moral choices is far from being simple. Due to the complexity of decisions faced by leaders, be that as it may, we sometimes catch wind of leaders who have settled on unscrupulous choices. I group these leaders into two. The first group is by a wide margin the majority.

It is those who are seen by others, and by themselves, as great individuals, however, who settle on choices that show to have destructive outcomes regardless of good aims. The second group is made up of individuals who deliberately break the standards and settle on unreasonable decisions, who do not have certain individual qualities, for example, moral character. These are in the minority.

When confronted with an intricate choice, it is human instinct to try to streamline it, to some way or another reframe the problem into one that we feel and perceive we can serenely solve. Oversimplifying the problem may lead to decision makers neglecting to consider all the potential results of a decision or to them missing critical information.

To maintain strategic distance to this pitfall one approach is to support every one of those with an enthusiasm in the problem at hand to talk about and examine it. Empowering a sound society in which difficult questions can be asked is fundamental to abstaining from improving the problem and settling on choices which end up having unanticipated and unsafe results.